THE WALLS CAME TUMBLING DOWN

JOSHUA 1–6 FOR CHILDREN

Written by Dave Hill

Illustrated by

Jim Roberts and Art Kirchhoff

ARCH Books

© 1967 CONCORDIA PUBLISHING HOUSE, ST. LOUIS, MISSOURI
CONCORDIA PUBLISHING HOUSE LTD., LONDON, E. C. 1
MANUFACTURED IN THE UNITED STATES OF AMERICA
ALL RIGHTS RESERVED
ISBN 0-570-06024-9

When God had led His people through
the desert long years past,
He told them of the Promised Land
He'd lead them to at last.

Now River Jordan lay ahead,
beyond that – Canaan Land,
their own to take as soon as God
would lead them with His hand.

God chose a man named Joshua
and gave him this command:
"Over Jordan lead My people
to the Promised Land."

But just across the river wide
sat high-walled Jericho.
So Joshua picked out two spies
and said to them: "You go
and see how strong the city is.
Come back and let us know.
For big, strong men live in that town,
and they will stand and fight!
So you two men must go and spy
on Jericho tonight!"

The spies reached Jericho by night
and quickly sneaked inside
the walls to have a look about.
But then a soldier cried:
"Who are you strangers over there?"

And they ran off to hide.

"Come here, you men – I'll help you hide!"
they heard a woman call.
They raced inside her house, which sat
upon the city wall.

"You men must hide," the woman said,
and Rahab was her name.
"Up on the roof – I'll hide you there.
I am so glad you came,
for all the folks here are afraid –
we hear of you, you see.
And I know God is on your side.
He gives you victory."

She covered them with mats of reeds
until the soldiers passed,
then brought them down and said to them:
"You'll have to leave here – fast!"

She set a basket on the floor
and took a rope – bright red –
and tied the basket to it tight.
"Now get inside!" she said.
"I'll let you down the city wall
and leave the rope to show
my house – so when your soldiers come,
they'll let my family go."

The spies ran back to Joshua
and happily cried out:

"The people are afraid of us!
We'll win without a doubt!"

But others shouted, "Where's the bridge?
Just see that water run!"

"God moved with us," said Joshua,
"in all things we have done.
And He will hold the waters back.
We march with morning sun."

At dawn the priests marched with the ark
down to the riverside.
The Ten Commandments, carved on stone,
were safely held inside.

They stopped to pray, then walked right in
and held the ark up high.
"A miracle!" the people cried,
for Jordan had gone dry!

Across the empty riverbed
the people marched all day.
Then Joshua, the general, said:
"Let us all kneel and pray
and thank the Lord for this good land
He gave to us today!"

Next day they marched to Jericho
and camped about the wall.
"It's high!"
  "And strong!"
    "And thick!"
      they said.
"But God will make it fall!"

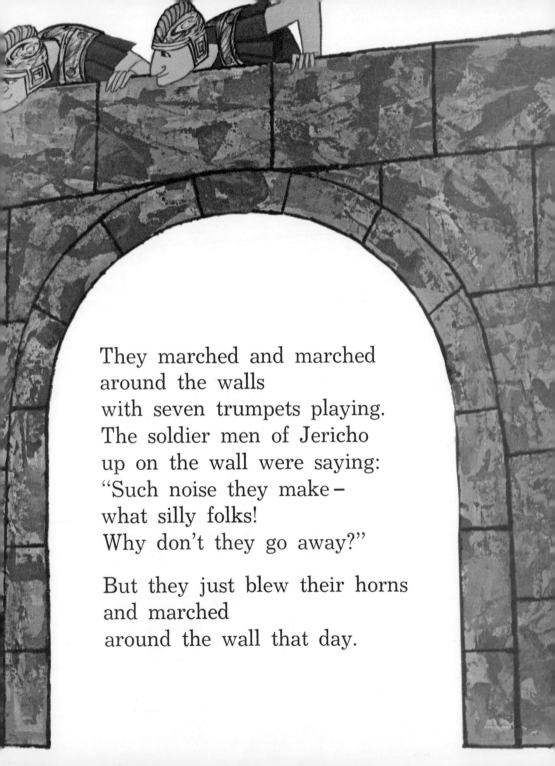

They marched and marched
around the walls
with seven trumpets playing.
The soldier men of Jericho
up on the wall were saying:
"Such noise they make –
what silly folks!
Why don't they go away?"

But they just blew their horns
and marched
around the wall that day.

For six long days they did the same;
then came the seventh day.

"Today we win," said Joshua.
"Let's hear your trumpets play!"

With trumpets loud the people marched
around the walls so high
for seven trips – and then they stopped
and raised a mighty cry!!!

A sound of thunder filled the land
and rumbled all around,

as mighty Jericho's great walls

CAME TUMBLING TO THE GROUND!

Said Joshua: "Go take the town,
but Rahab shall go free,
for now she wants to serve the Lord
with all her family."

"We have a home,"
   the people cried.
      "God gave us victory."

DEAR PARENTS:

The story of how the walls of Jericho came tumbling down is part of the great adventure of God's people.

God had called Abraham to leave his home and venture into the unknown. He promised him and his children a new homeland in the land of Canaan. At a later time his descendants became slaves in Egypt. After many years God led the Hebrews out of slavery. Forty years they wandered in the Sinai desert region. Only the next generation had the faith to venture into the land of Canaan, inhabited by "people greater and taller" than they, with "cities great and fortified up to heaven." (Deuteronomy 1:28)

God gave Joshua the faith to lead his people across the Jordan to possess Jericho, the fortress city at the entrance to the Promised Land. Now this homeless people had a home, a land in which they could freely develop into the kind of people God had in mind when He had chosen them to bear a blessing for all the nations of the earth. (Genesis 12:2-3)

Will you lead your child to see how our story fits into the plan of salvation God had for His people? Will you help him see that Joshua marched against Jericho on the strength of God's promise? Will you help your child believe that God has ways to pull down walls in our lives today?

THE EDITOR